celebrate♥

Girls Lit from Within:

A Guide to Life
Outside of the Girl Box

From the Founder and *Vision Keeper* of

Girls on the Run International

Molly Barker

This book is for you or you
wouldn't be reading it.
Nothing, over the course of our lifetime,
ever happens by accident.

Dedication

This book is dedicated to
my daughter, Helen, my son, Hank, and
all the really cool girls and coaches
in *Girls on the Run*.

You give so much to me and I thought it was
about time I write a book about what you've
taught me.

I am, without a doubt,
your biggest fan,

Molly B.

This book is possible because of many people who love me and practice the insights discussed in this book.

Richard Weiss, my life partner and best friend, believes in me so much that he published this book. Richard, I love you with all of my heart and am so blessed that you are a part of my life.

Helen Barker is 7 years old right now and was the best critic and most honest of all the people who read this book. She thinks this book is pretty cool. Helen, you are my soda pop and lifeline to heaven.

Hank Barker is 10 years old right now and about to enter middle school. He continues to provide the most enlightened insight of anyone I know. Hank, you are the voice of calm in our wild and crazy family.

Kristin and Sophia Weiss were the first two girls to read this book in its entirety. Their phone calls and votes of confidence made me feel really awesome! Kristin and Sophia, thank you for accepting me just the way I am.

Helen Harrill is my best friend and she edited this book. She is one of the first women who gave me permission to love myself. Helen, you are my greatest teacher.

Betty Gomes who has enough faith in me to put HER reputation on the line and copy edit this book, on the advice of a mutual friend. Betty, thank you for being so brave!

The staff at *Girls on the Run* gave me the go-ahead to write this book and take valuable time away from the office to put these thoughts down on paper. I'm so grateful to each of you for YOUR passion for what WE do.

My mom, while her body isn't around anymore, the light of her star exists and weaves its beautiful and golden way through absolutely every endeavor I undertake. This book is made up of the words she shared with me, not with her voice, but the way she lived her life. She remains, to this day, the most out of the "Girl Box" human being I have ever known. Mom----Hank, Helen and I are doing okay. We feel your presence every day. We love you.

If you are an adult and you are buying this book, there are a few things I'd like for you to know.

First of all, I think you are very cool for buying this book. The experience that I hope this book brings to the little girl in your life is the one I feel every time I am with her. I feel lighter, more beautiful and extremely grateful.

Secondly, I'd like to suggest that *you* read the book in its entirety. It's an easy read—maybe 45 minutes or so. This way you are prepared to discuss the insights. Even better, I've learned that if I actually practice these insights, I automatically become a better role model for my own children. The old adage goes, "practice what you preach." I try to live this mantra every day, not only for the girls in our program, but for my own two children.

Thirdly, if you have any concerns or comments, please don't hesitate to e-mail me at molly@girlsontherun.org. I want you to know that one of the most important facets to my own spiritual growth is that I remain accessible to the girls we serve. I never want to be out of reach or seen as if I have it totally all together. I don't! I'm just another parent/caregiver like you, trying to do my best in raising my children and impacting the world in a positive way. I thrive on constructive criticism (and, of course, positive feedback), so lay it on me!

Lastly, thank you for sharing my words and my thoughts with the little girl in your life. As *Girls on the Run* has gotten bigger, I've lost some of the intimate contact with the girls we serve, and I'm telling the honest truth when I share with you that this book is my attempt to reclaim some of that intimacy...connection...FUN! I've loved writing this book because in doing so, I've experienced many early morning moments with my Divine and have rediscovered the importance of practicing these principles so that I stay out of the "Girl Box."

Thanks and may the abundance that love brings, surround you.

Molly B.

Table of Contents

Chapter 1
Getting to Know Each Other

Chapter 1: Getting to Know Each Other

Let's get one thing straight, right off the bat.

I love you.

Okay...that may seem a little weird. I know what you're thinking. "She doesn't even know me!"

The truth is...I do know you. You are, after all, a *Girl on the Run*. You are vibrant. You are fun. You are honest. You are generally happy. You say what's on your mind. You are active. You are **Real**!

You are everything I want to be.

Ten years ago I started *Girls on the Run* for many reasons, but one of the most important reasons was this:

I knew that you would love me back.

Girls like you are usually pretty open-minded and accepting. I knew that you wouldn't make fun of me or put me down. I knew that when I was having a bad day, spending time with you would move me closer to a better mood.

I knew that you had the kind of love for life that I wanted. So, when I started *Girls on the Run*, it was a win-win kind of endeavor.

You get something out of it and so do I. Now don't get me wrong. I know life isn't always happy, joyous and free. It can be tough, nowadays, being a girl.

Sometimes we can be mean.

Sometimes we can really hurt each other's feelings.

Sometimes we feel ugly. Trying to feel beautiful about ourselves is a challenge when all we see in magazines are pictures of girls and women that have been created on a computer.

Sometimes we compare ourselves to those pictures and feel like we don't measure up.

Sometimes we feel dumb. Not every girl in the world can make straight A's, and when we don't, it's hard to find the "smarts" inside of us.

Sometimes we feel unpopular. We might feel like we don't fit in or we don't look right in our clothes. We might look in the mirror and wish that we could look like someone else.

I know you feel all of these things sometimes. Because, you know what? I do too. I'm just an older girl inside an older body. But my friends and I all struggle with the same kind of feelings. Even 40 year-olds want to be popular, sometimes.

When I started *Girls on the Run*, I had been living the life of the girl who never felt like she quite fit in. I never felt pretty enough, smart enough, sassy enough, fashionable enough...
I never felt like being myself was good enough.

And so when I was in about sixth grade, I went into the "Girl Box." The "Girl Box" is this imaginary place where many girls go around sixth grade. In the "Girl Box" we say farewell to the really cool girl that we are and we begin to try to be a girl we think will make us popular.

It all started when my best friend, Frances, started getting breasts and I didn't. Suddenly she was getting all kinds of attention from boys, and I felt left out. Nothing about me was any different than I had been the summer before, but I felt invisible. No one was talking to me anymore. No one was looking at me anymore.

I realized that if I started acting silly and flirtatious, instead of just being myself, I could get some of the attention Frances was getting. I cried a lot my sixth-grade year. I felt like girls would form groups and leave me out. One of the girls in my class even bullied me during P.E. by throwing the basketball at my face.

About four years later, when I was 15 years old, I

started running with my mom. My mom was one of the coolest women around. My mother and I were very close. The two of us would go running at 6:00 in the morning, before school. I can close my eyes now and feel the cool morning air on my face, feel the sweat as it would roll down the sides of my face, hear our breathing and the scuffle of our footsteps as they would hit the sidewalk, step for step.

I loved to run. Running for me was the one time during my day when I felt like I was my old self again. I didn't worry about what I looked like or what people thought about me. My mind would empty itself of all of my thoughts and I could rediscover the fun, energetic and genuine girl I had left behind in sixth grade... when I went into the "Girl Box."

I was myself again.

It's kind of weird, but it was also when I was about15, that I started doing some things that were really bad for me. I had my first cigarette, started going to parties and generally began acting like girls who were very lost in the "Girl Box."

Sadly, this lack of respect for myself began to get me the attention I had always wanted. I immediately became one of the popular girls. I suddenly, from an outsider's point of view, seemed to fit in.

Yet (and this is the **best** part about being old), I can look back over my life and gain something called **perspective**. That means I can look at the path my life has taken from a viewpoint that puts the experiences of my life into some kind of meaningful sequence. I can now look back and see that I was one of the saddest girls in the world. I cried a lot, spent too much time worrying about what I looked like, dieted a lot, fought with so called friends all the time and still, never had boyfriends who respected the real me. Even when I looked like I had it all together, I never really **felt** like I did.

I was a girl who had given up.

I was a girl who had given in.

I was a girl lost in the "Girl Box."

Fast forward 10 years. I am 25 years old and I've graduated from college. At that time I was teaching high school chemistry and competing in a very tough endurance sport called the triathlon.

A triathlon is where you swim, bike, and run... very long distances...and all in one day!!!

I was one of the best triathletes in the country. When I was training for and competing in triathlons, I felt free of the painful "Girl Box" that was defining who I was. I, for that brief part of my day, was the beautiful and free-spirited Molly I had been in fourth grade. I was happy, confident and joyous.

The rest of the time, however, I wasn't much fun

to be around. I was a difficult person. I gossiped a lot about people. I was angry. I hated the way I looked and I never followed through on promises I had made. I was very irresponsible and unreliable.

My family was beginning to worry about me.

Fast forward again, about seven years, to 1993. I had just completed an Ironman Triathlon. (That's a triathlon where you swim 2.4 miles in the ocean, bike 112 miles across very hot black lava fields in Hawaii and run 26.2 miles through rolling hills.) If you had looked at me back then, you would have seen one of the "fittest" looking people around. I was tan, lean, muscular, athletic and strong.

Yet, if you were to unzip my skin and turn me inside out...you would have seen that I was, on the inside, one of the unhealthiest people around. Behaviors I'd exhibited over the course of my "Girl Box" lifetime, up until then, were wreaking havoc on my health. My stomach was upset. My blood pressure was occasionally too high from unhealthy foods and stress and my lifestyle included very risky behaviors.

The most significant trait you would have noticed was I was "lightless." This means that the little light—the star—that shone inside of my soul was almost out. I felt so much shame about the person I had become…that I just quit allowing myself to feel anything. I was dull, sad and felt all alone.

I was depressed.

So on July 6, 1993, I called my big sister. I didn't know who else to call. (Aren't big sisters great?) I asked her to help me **feel** again. I asked her what I should do so I didn't feel so bad about myself all the time. I asked her to help get the painful "Girl Box" off of my life.

She lived far, far away so she couldn't actually hold me while I cried. But what she did was help me calm my tears. She talked to me in a soothing voice. She told me she loved me and that someday I would know why all of this was happening. Right before she hung up, she told me to curl up on the couch…right in the spot where I was…and go to sleep. "Things always look better in the morning, with a new sunrise and a fresh start."

Little did either of us know how right she was.

The next day was July 7, 1993. The day was hot. The day was sticky. The day was the day my life changed.

That afternoon around 4:00, I went for my daily run. There was a thunderstorm "brewing" off in the distance. Big black clouds were on the horizon and the wind was beginning to whip the leaves up off the pavement. The sun would peek through the clouds occasionally, and random drops of rain would escape from the sky.

I rounded a corner and began the last mile of my run, down a long and congested street.

Cars were whizzing by and the wind was really picking up.

When something very mysterious and beautiful began to happen.

I began to run really fast. The sounds of the traffic disappeared. I could hear my heart beating in my chest like the pounding of a loud drum. I could feel the soles of my feet lightly tapping the cement sidewalk under my feet. I smelled the hot summer pavement, fresh with wet rain. I felt the sweat from my effort, roll down the sides of my face, down my chest and down my back.

And then, it happened.

The "Girl Box" lifted right off of my shoulders. I had this sensation like I had left my body and was looking down at myself running. And who I saw, was the most beautiful woman in the world. She was vibrant. She was fun. She was real.

And she was ME!

I felt, for that moment, what you, and I, and all of the women of the world are capable of feeling…the most intense joy possible, because I was free of the suffocating "Girl Box." I rediscovered the girl I had left behind in sixth grade. For the first time since sixth grade, I felt comfortable in my skin.

I cried, right there on that busy street, and realized that I was crying tears of joy… something I had never done. I realized that to be a content girl, I needed to get out of that "Girl Box" and do everything I could to help girls either get out of the dreaded box, or better yet, NEVER GO IN!

That's where YOU come in. Three years later I started *Girls on the Run*. In 1996, I wrote the first set of lessons, tried them out with a group of girls at Charlotte Country Day School and the rest is history.

That's why this book is for you. I started *Girls on the Run* in an effort to help you feel like you never have to go into the "Girl Box." But what I've learned over the course of the last 10 years, since I started *Girls on the Run* is this; I think YOU know more about how to stay out of the "Girl Box" than I do, because you aren't in it yet.

You just aren't old enough to see it. Remember that word **perspective**? Older people have the privilege of having perspective from the simple fact that we are older. You can't really have perspective until you've lived a good number of years.

So what I thought would be cool…would be if we made a deal. Since you and all of your girlfriends in *Girls on the Run* have taught me so much about how to stay out of the "Girl Box" over the last several years, I thought my gift back to you…would be to add **perspective** to it. This means I will put it all together in some kind of sensible sequence so you can look at what you've taught me, from my adult point of view.

This way you can practice the things you are doing NOW, that keep you out of the "Girl Box"...so that you actually NEVER GO IN!!!

This book has a total of eight chapters: this one and seven more. Chapters 2 through 7 are the six insights you have given me...small tasks that if performed daily will keep you out of the "Girl Box"...for the rest of your life! I learned these by watching you and hearing what you do to stay true to the very cool person that you are, right now!

The eighth chapter is a summary chapter and puts chapters 1-7 into perspective. (I'll be using that word a lot!)

So............girlfriend!

Are you ready?

All right then. Fasten that seat belt and let's get this party started!

Chapter 2
You Are Lit From Within

Chapter 2: You are "Lit from Within"

To kick off this chapter, I've got a great story for you. I was flying to Chicago, Illinois, to lead a *Girls on the Run* training. When we start a *Girls on the Run* in a new city, I always go to the city to teach the adults there all about how to get *Girls on the Run* "up and running!" I was wandering my way through the Chicago O'Hare airport—which is huge, by the way— and couldn't find the woman who was there to pick me up. I had never met her or even seen a picture of her. I was making my way through the **very busy** terminal and was going up an escalator, with all of my baggage, when I saw a woman on the opposite side going down. She was smiling, full of energy, making eye contact with those around her and happy. She was healthy, vibrant and easy to spot! She was, as the expression goes, "lit from within." The star that was right there in the middle of her heart seemed to be shining from her body. I knew she was Kris, the woman who was picking me up. I knew this because most women and girls connected to *Girls on the Run* have that same look. They are "lit from within."

I took a chance, and hollered across the terminal. "Kris. Kris Anderson?"

The woman turned toward me, smiled and waved. We had found each other!

Now, I know we can't always **feel** "lit from within." Sometimes it's hard to stay enthusiastic about life. We all have tough days.

On the days when I'm feeling sad or "unlit" I love going to *Girls on the Run*, because when I show up, you are usually "lit from within." There is this special spark about you that never goes away.

Remember that very special day in my life, while out on a run I climbed out of the "Girl Box?" What I realize now, with some of that **perspective** I'm talking a lot about, is that during that run, I unplugged from the negative messages of the "Girl Box" and plugged into an entirely new way of thinking that is out of the "Girl Box." Being plugged into this positive energy is what makes us girls who are "lit from within."

So I started doing this cool visualization. (That's where you make a picture of something you want to happen, with your imagination). ***Every time I start to feel afraid that I won't be good enough at something or when I begin to feel myself listening to the negative messages of the "Girl Box" (when I'm comparing myself to the way other girls look or the things they have)***, I do this visualization. It helps me find that spark inside myself again so I stay "lit from within."

Here is what I do:

I picture that I have an electrical socket in the top of my brain. You know, like the one where you might plug in your curling iron or your hair dryer. I then picture that I have a cord plugged into it. Like an electrical cord, except this cord is special because I can see into it and I can see what the stuff going through this cord looks like. The substance in it is very slow-moving. It is brown, black and mucky and has the texture of peanut butter. If it made a sound, the sound would be a thick, glugging, "glub, glub, glub" sound. This yucky stuff that goes down into my brain through this " Girl Box" cord goes down into my body and begins to dim the spark—the bright star—that is right where my heart is (and is, by the way at the center of who I am). That beautiful spark begins to pop and fizz and slowly, like a dying star, begins to disappear. The message of this brown, globby cord that is seeping its way into me, says things like, "You aren't pretty enough," or "You aren't smart enough," or "You aren't sassy enough," or "You aren't popular enough," or "You aren't thin enough." Basically the message of this cord is "Molly, you just will never, EVER be good enough."

At this point in my visualization, I take a minute and think about how I feel. I become aware of how being plugged into this kind of cord isn't good for me. It makes me sad, angry, depressed and closed in on myself. It doesn't allow others to see the bright light of who I really am. This cord suffocates my star instead of helping it to shine brighter.

I then reach up with my left hand and unplug that cord, right out of the top of my head. I really do this. If you were watching me, you would see me *really* reach my left hand up to my head, grab hold of an imaginary cord and pull it out of the top of my head. I then take that cord and toss it (with enthusiasm) behind me! (Okay, I'll admit, it might look crazy, but I do this anyway! Hey, I'm unplugging from the negative "Girl Box," and don't care anymore if I look a little bit crazy!)

I then reach up toward the sky with my right hand and grab another cord (imaginary, of course) and pop it into the imaginary socket in the top of my head. I even will say, out loud, the word "*POP*" as I pop this new cord into my head! This cord, girlfriend, is the "*Girls on the Run* cord," the one I plugged into on my life-changing run. I can see into this cord and the liquid in it is sparkly and bubbly and full of color. If this liquid were to make a noise it would sound like bubbling water running over a beautiful mountain creek. The liquid in this cord bubbles down onto the spark inside of me, which makes me the wonderful Molly I am, and begins to pop and fizz and shine brighter. The light right there, the star of my heart begins to send out so much light that now I have light coming out of my eyes, my ears, my fingertips and my voice. When I walk, light is bouncing off of my footsteps and hair and even leaves a trail of light behind me!

And the message of this cord, the *Girls on the Run* cord, is "You are beautiful just the way you are. Molly, you ARE good enough. You really ARE quite fabulous!!"

At this point in my visualization, I just see how that feels. I automatically feel stronger, more confident and more comfortable in my skin. I feel my body stand up a bit taller, my shoulders are back and my head is held high. I become "lit from within."

I can then walk into just about any situation and feel okay about myself. I don't compare myself to others girls, but I also don't put other girls down. I am just me, **content** with who I am.

So now you and I have finished Chapter 2! We've learned one little tip we can use **any time we begin to feel the "Girl Box" come down over the spark of our spirit**.

So will you promise me that you will use this visualization any time you need it? I will. This will be OUR pact, between two girls, you and me— a pact which will keep me from going back in the "Girl Box" and you from ever going there. Okay?

All right, superstar...on to Chapter 3!

Chapter 3
Gratitude is an Attitude

Chapter 3: Gratitude is an Attitude

Sometimes when that "Girl Box" cord is making its way back into my brain, I find myself complaining a lot. I'm not happy with the way I look. I hate the clothes I own. My job is too tiring. I wish I had more money. I wish I had more free time. I wish I had something that I don't have.

This ungrateful attitude is an obvious sign that I'm headed right back to the "Girl Box." In the "Girl Box," instead of being grateful for what I have, I get caught in the mindset of wishing I had more. I wish I was prettier, more popular and had more friends.

But when I watch you at *Girls on the Run*, you celebrate every amazing thing your body can do. Remember when you ran your first 5K? Or if you haven't run one yet, isn't it wonderful that you can run or walk at all? Girls like you are grateful for what they are able to do. Without even trying, you have an attitude of gratitude.

Every little new thing you get or every new thing you experience is exciting and fun. You don't compare yourselves to other girls, like adults do. I had forgotten what real gratitude was like until I started coming to *Girls on the Run* and had the opportunity to feel it all over again with you.

To make sure I keep an attitude of gratitude, here is another easy task I perform every day: I make a gratitude list.

At night time I take several minutes and write down in a spiral notebook (my journal actually, but I'll get to that in Chapter 4), at least 10 things for which I am grateful.

Here, I'll share one of my lists with you:

My Gratitude List for May 29, 2006

I am grateful for:
1. My children, Hank and Helen;
2. My best friend, Richard;
3. My best friend's children, Sophia and Kristin;

4. My health;
5. My awesome job at *Girls on the Run*;
6. My sweet little dogs, Lacey and Abigail;
7. My blonde hair;
8. My tomboyish-like personality;
9. My open mind;
10. My kind heart.

I will share with you the best part about writing a gratitude list. I IMMEDIATELY feel content. Instead of seeing the world through eyeglasses that have me wanting more....I'm suddenly seeing the world through eyeglasses that allow me to see my life as full.

There is an expression that says "You can either see the glass as half full or as half empty." Girls in the "Girl Box" tend to see the glass as half empty. They want more.

Girls out of the "Girl Box" tend to see the glass as half full. They are thrilled that they have anything in the glass at all!

So now, we know how to do task number two. Every night, write out a gratitude list with the top 10 things in your life for which you are grateful. Put the list next to your bed. In the morning before you roll out of bed, re-read the list.

Hop up and out of that bed for a day filled with an attitude of gratitude.

While the task is easy, you still have to do it to make it happen.
I promise to write out a gratitude list every night, if you will! All right then, let's shake on it.

Now, on to Chapter 4!

Chapter 4
Journal

Chapter 4: Journal

When I was in third grade my big sister, Helen, gave me a diary. The green diary had a plastic shiny cover on it with the words "MY DIARY" written in cursive across the front. A tiny key opened and closed a very small lock allowing me to lock in everything that I chose to write on those pages. At the top of each page was the date, and I would always write in it, each evening...like I was talking to a friend. I would share with my diary what I had done during that day. I also wrote down some feelings about what I had done.

The next Christmas, I got another diary from my sister. Getting a diary from her every Christmas became a tradition. I always looked forward to what it would look like, the size of it, the texture of the pages.

When I was in middle school, my sister realized that a small diary wouldn't work anymore, because in middle school I had many more thoughts, fears and "things" I needed to write about. So she gave me a journal...

Every night I would take a good 15 to 30 minutes to write in my journal. Each page had lines on it so that I could guide my pen across the white pages, leaving my fears, thoughts and comments there for me to review later.

Recently, I found one of those journals and read through some of my thoughts. At the time I was in eighth grade and was at Cape Cod with a family, serving as their on-call baby sitter.

I was beginning to develop breasts and wrote all about how strange I felt wearing a two-piece bathing suit at the beach. Of course, now that I'm older I read these words and find some wonderful memories in them. But at the time, the journal served as the only safe place for me to write my fears and concerns about moving from the space of "little girl" to "adult woman."

Suggestion number three, therefore, to staying out of the "Girl Box" is to **keep a very private**

journal. You don't have to spend any money on a journal. You can take pieces of notebook paper and attach them at the three holes by tying three small pieces of yarn or ribbon into three pretty bows. Decorate the front cover with whatever small illustrations you think will make it beautiful.

When you take time each evening, best right before bed, to write in your journal, remember to just let your thoughts flow. A journal will only keep you out of the "Girl Box" if you don't worry about what you are writing and just write. Start with one certain theme…like friendship…and then just start writing. One thought will lead to another and before you know it…in 10 minutes you will have several pages of what has been in your mind, down on paper.

Before you finish your journal time, go back and read what you've written. Think about what you have written and then see if you can come up with one sentence that describes the main idea of what you have written.

The most important part about keeping a journal, is to keep your journal well-hidden and for **your eyes only.** Don't leave it out for your little brother to find or even your parents to discover. If you are worried other people might find your journal, you are very likely to not write down what your **real** thoughts are and will end up writing what you think others may want to read. This will completely defeat the purpose of the journal.

My mom once wrote in the cover of one of the journals she gave me for my birthday, *"Find a safe place to write down all of your secrets. Then your secrets are no longer imprisoned... and neither is your soul."*

Let's both promise to keep a journal, okay? Will you make yours or buy one? I like the idea of making my own...decorating it with my style and hiding it in a safe place in my room. For me, I think I'll put it under the mattress on my bed. How about you? Where will you hide yours?

Chapter 5
Meditate

Chapter 5: Meditate

All right....what I'm going to talk to you about in this chapter may seem a bit weird, but I learned all about it by watching you.

As we both know, *Girls on the Run* is a crazy and active hour of fun! There is a ton of talking, movement and giggling. By the end of the hour we both are fully energized, in love with life, talkative and sweaty!

But sometimes, I've watched you come to *Girls on the Run* and you've had a rough day at school. Maybe one of your friends hurt your feelings or maybe you didn't do so hot on a test.

Your energy level seems to be a bit subdued.

I feel this way sometimes, too. I can't seem to find my normal upbeat self and I'm just **not** in the mood to be silly and talkative.

I've noticed that when you are like that, you

naturally (and healthily) go through the motions of the lesson, but you are somehow "inside yourself." You seem to be looking inward instead of being actively engaged with those around you. You seem to be, even in the presence of all of those girls around you, taking some "quiet" time for yourself.

Because you are out of the "Girl Box," you don't worry about what your friends will think about you when and if you need to take this time for yourself. You just take it. You take it if you are in a group or if you are at home. You seem to understand how important it is to just shut out all of the noise of the world around you and rest.

I respect this about you so much and have learned that this is one of the most important activities I can do to stay out of the "Girl Box."

Quiet Time. Think about it. Everywhere we go there is noise. We are always doing something. We wake up, eat breakfast, get dressed, go to school, spend time with others, leave school, go to *Girls on the Run* or some other extracurricular activity, come home, eat dinner, do homework and then go to bed.

WHEW. I just got tired writing out all of the activities!

As we get older, the many tasks we have to perform get more complicated and often involve more people. I'm a single mother with two kids, a full-time job, a house to manage and a life to live. I'm driving here, there and everywhere and half the time, by the end of the day, I haven't stopped long enough to consider what I'm thinking, feeling or doing.

Quiet time is not a natural part of my adult day. I often feel pulled in so many directions that I don't take time to pull inward, as you do, when you are tired, stressed or crazy.

So guess what I have to do? I have to **MAKE** quiet time. Instead of waiting for it to magically appear in my day, I sit quietly in a big yellow chair in my breakfast room and **meditate.** I meditate every morning, before my kids wake up.

I'll bet you are laughing out loud right now because you are picturing me sitting in the chair with my legs crossed and my hands in some funny position while I'm chanting **OHMMMMM.** Close, but not really. The way a person meditates can't be defined by anyone else. Meditation has to be defined by you and done in a way that is comfortable for you. Sometimes people pray during meditation. Other people sit quietly and think about what they have to do in their day. Others try to clear their minds completely of any thoughts. (I personally do a combination of praying and clearing my mind.)

My mom used to meditate every morning. I would wake up, tip-toe downstairs and find her listening to calming music and sitting in a chair with her hands crossed in her lap. I knew this was sacred time for her…so I would tip-toe back to my room or to the kitchen.

Here are some pointers to using your meditation time efficiently:

- Try to meditate first thing in the morning, before you are dressed for the day. The quiet time first thing in the day really helps kick the day off with your thoughts together and your emotions in sync with one another;

- Try to always meditate in the same spot. Pick a favorite place...maybe on the floor of your room; maybe in a chair in your room. Most people avoid meditating on their beds, because guess what happens? They end up falling back asleep and you definitely don't want to do that!

- Sit comfortably with your legs relaxed and your hands resting in your lap. Try to pick a position that you can hold for at least five minutes. I usually sit with my legs in a criss-cross position and my hands are gently folded in my lap. My head is upright and slightly down.

- Close your eyes.
- Now, here's where what **you** want to do, comes next. I tend to "look" at the backs of my eyelids, with my eyes shut, and see what I see. Sometimes I see what looks like the outline of my eye. Sometimes I see light. Sometimes I see black.
- Meditation experts say that if you repeat one word over and over, inside your mind, you can really clear your mind of all of those negative "Girl Box" messages and open your mind to more positive messages.
- The word I repeat is my favorite word "*love.*" I just say it over and over and any time another word, image or idea enters my thoughts I just gently nudge it out of my imagination, with the word love.
- Eventually I'm in a very peaceful state. I'm breathing very deeply. I almost lose track of where my hands, arms, legs and feet are resting on the chair.
- After a few minutes (sometimes five and

sometimes 30), I open my eyes and say
a prayer.
- Remember, the point of meditation is
  not to psych you up for the day, but
  to **center** you for the day. Centering
  yourself means surrounding yourself with
  thoughts that keep you focused on the
  goodness of the world around you.

When I take time to meditate in the morning,
here's what I gain throughout the day:

I feel lit from within.
I am open-minded and less judgmental of
myself and others.
I gain insight. If a problem in my life has been
really bugging me, I gain insight on how to
handle the problem.

If you are a little bit weirded out right now, I
understand. Meditation has gotten a bad rap.
Usually, we think people who are a bit *different*
meditate. I can assure you that while I may be
a bit different (in a really fun and crazy way!!!!),

meditation is something that a lot of people are doing nowadays.

Go ahead and try meditating, for at least three weeks. You can "report" in your journal how meditation makes you feel. You can keep track of the difference in how your days go, when you meditate, and when you don't meditate.

I think you will notice a tremendous difference. Meditation will help you see the world through more open eyes and a much more open heart!

So we've done it. We've made it through Chapter 5! Now on to Chapter 6 and one of the most challenging insights yet!

Chapter 6
Make Amends

Chapter 6: Make Amends

One of the hardest things to do is admit when we are wrong. Girls in the "Girl Box" have an even more difficult time admitting they are wrong.

Think about it. The message of the "Girl Box" is "you are not good enough." Therefore girls trapped inside that dreadful box can't admit when, they are wrong...because to do so would be admitting that they really aren't perfect...and therefore in their minds they think they really *aren't* good enough.

I would argue with that idea. Whenever someone has done something wrong and they apologize for it, I actually feel closer to that person. I admire them a lot for having the courage to admit that they are wrong and even more so for apologizing for it.

Something I try to do every day is make amends to those whom I may have harmed. I love when

I can go to sleep with my thoughts not tangled up in any negative energy around a lie I may have told or a girl I may have gossiped about.

Let's face it. You aren't perfect and neither am I. We ARE going to do something wrong.

For example, as much as I'd like to think I don't ever gossip, sometimes I do. If I said something about someone that wasn't true, I try as soon as I realize that I was dishonest to call the person with whom I gossiped and let her know that "I'm not sure that what I said was actually true. I think I just got caught up in all the gossip of it and I want to let you know that I didn't mean any of what I said. That was 'Girl Box' behavior and you deserve better than that from me. I'm so sorry."

Even moms get caught in a lie. This past week, I took some lip gloss out of my daughter's room without asking for it. I carried it to the car with me. When Helen got in the car, she asked if the lip gloss in the console between our seats belonged to her. I stumbled through some mumbling response about how I didn't know how that got there and well...I'm not sure if it was hers or not. Of course, Helen knew it was hers and so did I. The problem was I had taken it from her room without asking and I was embarrassed for my disrespectful behavior— especially toward my own daughter!

I realized how very wrong I was, but it took me almost two hours to work up the nerve to call Helen (she was at her Dad's house) and apologize for not being honest. I also apologized for taking the lip gloss from her room without asking.

Apologizing wasn't all I needed to do. The next step was to make amends, which means I had to really make "the situation right." I went to the drug store and bought her a new lip gloss. I had used some of hers and I owed her what I had used without asking. I put the new lip gloss back in her room and let her know it was there.

To be totally honest with you, I don't think there

has been anything, over the course of my lifetime that hurt ME quite so much as lying to Helen. I'm her mother and I realize that I am a role model for her. Yet, I also realize that role models aren't perfect and my making amends to her was demonstrating to her how girls out of the "Girl Box" behave.

One day, Helen will remember that I apologized to her.

Take a minute, right now, and shut your eyes. I want you think about any friend or family member whom you've harmed in the past. How do you feel on the inside when you think about what you did to hurt them? I know that when I have done something that has really hurt someone else OR when I've told a lie, it eats me up on the inside. The wrong that I did doesn't just go away. It sits inside my emotional soul and won't go away until I somehow release it. That's why apologizing to someone can be so powerful! Saying you are sorry is one indirect way to pull the negative cord out of the top of your head. Apologizing lets you be human and to admit that you aren't perfect!

People who apologize when they have done something wrong are expressing a very out of the "Girl Box" character trait called **humility.** Humility isn't the same thing as being humiliated. Being humiliated happens when you fall down in the cafeteria or spill your milk all down the front of your shirt when you are out with friends.

Humility is showing those around you that you aren't perfect. Humility is having the ability to laugh at yourself. A **humble** person shows humility.

It's never too late to apologize or to make amends. Tonight when you are writing in your journal, why don't you make a list of those folks whom you have harmed and over the course of the next several weeks try to apologize to them? Sometimes our apologies may hurt someone more than help them. In that case, you will just have to let your apology go and try to forgive yourself for what you did.

However, if you can apologize and your apology won't hurt the person, go ahead and do it! You will be amazed at how good you feel. You'll be able to look all those with whom you come into contact, directly in the eye. You will feel like your step is a lot lighter. You won't be carrying around the burden of your lie or harmful behavior.

You will feel like the cool girl you really are...the girl I know in *Girls on the Run*...the girl very much OUT OF THE "GIRL BOX!!!"

Before I close out this chapter, I thought I might share with you a concept that helps keep me on the "honest path." The concept is called **Karma.** Karma is the notion that when we do something good, even when no one is watching us, the "good we did" begins to circulate in and all throughout our lives. Eventually all the good we do in our lives, comes back to us.

Here is an example of how this principle might work. Let's pretend I'm walking from the parking lot at the YMCA to the building itself. On the way, I see a squashed Coke can sitting in the parking lot. Instead of just walking right over it, I pick it up and place it in the trash can on the way into the building.

I have no idea how my simple act of picking up the Coke can may have helped someone else. Perhaps a car was going to roll over the rough edges of the can and get a flat tire. Or maybe a little kid was going to try to kick the can and may have cut her foot on it. The parking lot is part of my life and my surroundings and it is my responsibility to keep it clean.

Simple and kind acts like this, built up over a lifetime, create a positive energy that swirls all around us. People like to be with people who have that kind of positive energy. Performing kind acts such as picking up trash or apologizing when I've done something wrong are other indirect ways of plugging into the positive out of the "Girl Box" cord.

What's really cool at this point (you've probably already noticed), is how all of the insights we've already discussed are beginning to rely on each other! You need to unplug from the negative cord in order to stay out of the "Girl Box," but sometimes we do stuff that puts us in the box, so we have to journal and meditate to figure out what to do to get out of the box. After journaling and meditating we may realize that we owe someone an apology! All of these positive behaviors create a Karma in our lives that surrounds us with positive energy, which then attracts positive people who help us stay out of the "Girl Box" because they love us just the way we are!

Whew! I'm always amazed how everything and every person are connected. ***How I live my life is actually creating the life that I am living!***

Enough of this deep stuff! Let's move on to one of my favorite insights!!! Onward, girlfriend! Chapter 7 awaits!

Chapter 7
Dance

Chapter 7: Dance

If there is one thing that a *Girl on the Run* does more often than anything else, it's DANCE. You dance on your way to the track. You dance your way around the track. You dance when you see your best friend. You dance in the car. (We call that "jukin'" in my house.)

What amazes me about you is the way your body moves when you dance. You are totally uninhibited in your skin. I watch you dance, whether you are serious or silly, and I marvel at how beautiful you appear to be.

You are IT!

You are LIGHT!

You are SPIRIT!

As you know, we do our crazy energy awards at *Girls on the Run*, when someone does something wonderful OR when one of our teammates needs some help unplugging from the negative cord and popping into the positive one. The energy awards are fun, silly, goofy, and are like miniature dances. Each energy award incorporates everything that I believe makes *Girls on the Run*, the fun and life-changing program that it is.

Think about it! How can you possibly remain sad, angry or depressed when you do a loud, crazy and joyous "Superstar!" (Just in case you don't know what a Superstar is, it looks something like this. You put both arms down, straight at the sides of your body and on the count of 1, 2, 3 you leap up in the air, bend your left knee and plant that left foot in front of you on the floor, while at the same time, lifting your right foot back to land in a stance behind you, that stabilizes you. Your hands both go straight up in the air at the same time and you shout out "**SUPERSTAR**"...all of this beautifully coordinated to occur at the same moment.

If you don't "get it" from my description, next

time we see each other, make sure you ask me about it. I would love to show you!

Thanks to you, I dance all the time. I dance in the car a lot, which by the way embarrasses my kids sometimes, but they love me enough to let me do it! I dance in my house with or without kids there...often I'm alone. I'll put some good music on and dance all over the house: up the stairs, while I'm dressing, while I'm fixing dinner and while I'm on my way out of the door for a run!

Dancing in some goofy way is liberating. Dancing is the easiest way to show my human side to those around me. I feel totally comfortable in my skin.

If you aren't accustomed to dancing, don't panic. You can grow into it. Start small. Maybe while you are in the car and your mom is driving, just tap your foot on the floor. Eventually do the "foot tap" a little bit bigger. Next you might add a snap, clap or some fun movement with your head!

If you are really bold, just go for it! I dare you to dance right now. Get up….NOW!!! Put this book down and dance, wherever you are, RIGHT THIS MINUTE!

Don't come back to this book for at least one minute. Dance for the whole minute!

I'll be waiting……

(I'm waiting.)

(Still waiting.)

(A few more seconds.)

Okay, tell me. How do you feel? Good, right?

See? You just can't stay in the "Girl Box" if you are dancing. JOY is what dancing is really all about. Dancing is **the** expression of JOY. JOY for who you are; JOY for the life you are creating: JOY for living your life outside of the "Girl Box."

Thanks to the time I spend with you in *Girls on the Run*, I now have another tool to use when I find that I'm lowering the "Girl Box" down over my life. I dance so hard, so vigorously and so joyously that it can't possibly stay on me!

We all need to dance. No matter how old we are, no matter the size of our bodies, no matter where we live or how much money we have. We need to unite as sisters and DANCE like there is no tomorrow!

So get on with your beautiful self and ***dance, SISTER, DANCE!!!!***

Chapter 8
Love

Chapter 8: Love

All right, friend. We've made it to the last chapter, the one that pulls together the six insights into some kind of **perspective**. (Are you tired of that word yet?)

Let's review.

The six insights were:

YOU:

- Are lit from within;
- Possess an attitude of gratitude;
- Journal;
- Meditate;
- Make amends;
- Dance.

I was on an airplane, not too long ago, flying home from a *Girls on the Run* 5k event. I started writing down the insights and was struck immediately by the deeper trait that each of the six insights brings.

Here they are:

YOU:

- Are lit from within; therefore you are **CONTENT**.
- Possess an attitude of gratitude; therefore you are **GRATEFUL**.
- Meditate; therefore you are **CENTERED.**
- Journal; therefore you are **SELF-AWARE.**
- Make amends; therefore you are **HUMBLE**.
- Dance; therefore you are **JOYOUS**.

Now here's the funny part. I couldn't stop there. I started thinking about how possessing each of these traits helps you and me stay out of the "Girl Box" and helps keep our spirits "lit from within!"

And look what came next!

CONTENT

JOYOUS

GRATEFUL

HUMBLE

CENTERED

SELF-AWARE

I can tell you right now, that any girl who is able to possess these six qualities that shine out from each point of this star, is going to do just fine in this lifetime. The light from within her will shine so brightly that anyone—yes, ANYONE—that comes into contact with that will be so warmed by it that he/she will want to spend time in it.

This is called the power of attraction. I'm not talking about the kind of attraction that girls have for boys or boys have for girls. I'm talking about the kind of attraction that connects two people, whether they are a boy or girl or man or woman to each other in a real and genuine way.

This kind of attraction can change the way a person feels about life. I sometimes like to imagine that if all of the people in the world felt this kind of light, warmth and safety with each other, there would be no wars. There would be no murders. There would be very little pain.

Perspective, however, has taught me that we cannot truly celebrate the warmth of sunshine on a beautiful fall morning, unless we have felt the cold of dark clouds on a windy and bitter winter night.

If I could somehow teach you how to know the warmth of life outside of the "Girl Box" without your ever having to go into the shadow of it, I would. But I know that part of growing up and becoming a wise and light-filled woman means there will be times in your life when you will feel the painful box darken the world in which you live.

But, my sweet friend, what I also know, is that you have the tools to get outside of that box, anytime you choose to use them.

I know this because you have given them to me and I have written them in this book! You have shown me the wonder of life outside of the box, each and every time I meet you, spend time with you, and celebrate you.

You have helped me rediscover the power of being content, grateful, centered, self-aware, humble and joyous.

You have given back to me what I lost when I went into the "Girl Box" and what I was so painfully looking for inside of it.

You have given me **LOVE**!

The love I'm talking about is a very powerful kind of love. This kind of love just doesn't happen. We have to *make it* happen. You can't be "in" this kind of love. You have to actively create it from the energy you get from the sparkly, glittery and positive cord.

This kind of love is SO powerful that it can inspire:

- advertisers to use images of real girls whom we can aspire to be;

- girls to treat each other with respect, lift each other up and feel safe in each other's company;

- boys to treat us with respect and see us as the beautiful girls we are on the inside;

- those who have problems with their body image to seek help;

- those who feel left out to step into our circle where they are welcome;

- those who started smoking or drinking, to stop and those who never have, to never start;

- those who want to be like us, to simply be themselves;

- world leaders to seek peace instead of war;
- all of the women and men of the world to live in the light of love and step away from the shadow of fear.

Your love, my love, OUR love, is just that powerful.

The love you have given me is the kind of love that fuels the light of each and every point on each and every star, of each and every YOU.

So, in closing, let me share a very special story with you.

Several seasons ago, on a cloudy and cold day at *Girls on the Run*, I decided to walk a lap with each girl. I usually hand out the game pieces and stand in one place, but today, my assistant coach took on the "handing out the game pieces" job. At some point during the hour, I ended up walking a lap with a really cool girl (all of you are cool!) named Madeleine.

Madeleine was in fourth grade at the time and is still one of my best friends. She is one of the wisest people I know

With the wind whipping up the dead leaves of autumn, all around us, and the sky getting dark far away on the horizon, I asked…

"Madeleine, how is it that you and I ended up together? What happened so that you and I have been given the chance to know each other? How does all of that work? How did we both get so lucky?"

Madeline thought for several seconds—small puffs of warm air exiting her mouth, with each step.

And then she spoke—with the assurance of someone who has absolutely NO doubt about the words to follow. "Well it's like this," she said. "God has an idea. But he has a problem because he somehow needs to get that idea down to Earth. So to solve this problem, he wraps a body around the idea, and then brings the body down to Earth. If the idea is a really big one, he wraps two or three or lots of bodies around the idea, so that the really big idea can get here. That's how we get our gifts and talents. They are God's tools to help us get the idea out of our bodies and onto Earth."

I took her hand, slowed our walk to a stroll and knew that this would be a moment I would never forget. I realized, right then and there, that Madeleine had explained exactly what this whole book has been trying to explain. That at the center of our six pointed-star...you know the one with all of the traits necessary to stay out of the "Girl Box?"...lies an idea: **THE** idea that each of our bodies wraps itself around so that we can come down here to Earth and spend our lives, sharing it with others.

AND what lies at the center of each and every "idea" inside of each and every person is the most important and most powerful force in the world: **LOVE**...the love that I talked about before, which exists between you and me and all of the girls in *Girls on the Run*.

This love is so beautiful, sparkly and pure and it makes YOUR star, YOUR life, YOUR eyes, YOUR words, YOUR voice, and YOUR smile shine so brightly.

I want you to know that your love for me has been SO powerful that it has actually changed me. I am a better person because of your love. I shine more brightly because of it. I feel more confident, happier and like myself a lot, because of your love.

Your love has helped me love myself!

So thanks so much for sharing it with me.

I've had fun spending time with you. What's really cool is how we can have time together any time we want it by just opening up this book and reading it again, over and over. I figure that whenever I start to step into the "Girl Box" I can always turn to these words and the insights of this book and automatically feel better about myself.

So let's promise to each other that we will revisit this book, whenever we feel like the "Girl Box" is trying to put out the spark of who we are. This way we will both always stay "lit from within."

You take care of yourself, okay?

I love you,

Molly B.

Girls on the Run is a non-profit prevention program that encourages preteen girls to develop self-respect and healthy lifestyles through running. Our curricula address all aspects of a blossoming girl-spirit: their physical, emotional, mental, social and spiritual well-being.

Girls on the Run International is the parent organization of more than 150 Girls on the Run councils across the United States and Canada. Girls on the Run International establishes, trains and supports a network of community-level councils with local volunteers. The volunteers serve as role models to the girls through coaching the 12-week, 24 lesson curricula. The curriculum is delivered in these areas through after-school programs, recreation centers and other non-profit settings.

Help make a difference in the lives of girls everywhere and check us out at www.girlsontherun.org or call 800-901-9965.

Who is Molly Barker?

Molly Barker is a visionary whose personal mission is "to positively impact all those with whom I come into contact." The four time Hawaii Ironman triathlete, founded *Girls on the Run*® in Charlotte, North Carolina, in 1996. Molly began running at the age of 15—an age when she found herself stuck in the "Girl Box," when only girls who were a certain size with a certain beauty were popular; when girls who wanted to fit in had to mold their bodies and their personalities to fit the requirements of the box.

Molly kept running. Years later, on July 7, 1993, she took off on a sunset run and found the inspiration that grew into *Girls on the Run*®. Using her background in counseling and teaching, her personal recovery from alcoholism, along with research on adolescent issues, she developed the earliest version of the 12-week

24-lesson curriculum with the help of 13 brave girls at Charlotte Country Day School. The next session 26 girls showed up, then 75, and so the program grew.

In 1998, Runner's World, a national running magazine, awarded Molly its "Golden Shoe Award" for contributions to the community through running. That brief mention in Runner's World brought Molly calls from across the country and Canada. In 2000, Molly decided to share her brainchild with the world, and *Girls on the Run*, International®, a 501(c) (3) nonprofit, was born.

Today, there are *Girls on the Run*® programs in over 130 cities across North America, with tens of thousands of girls and women participating. In 2006, *Girls on the Run*® and New Balance will host over 50 end-of-season races across the United States and Canada. People, Runner's World, O Magazine, Running Times, MSNBC, ABC News, NBC News, NPR, ESPN, Forbes, CNN News and countless other newspapers and television shows have featured Molly and the program. Corporate sponsors for *Girls on the Run* International include New Balance Athletic Shoe and Apparel Company, Kellogg's Frosted Flakes and Goody's Hair Accessories.

With the success of her book, *Girls on Track, A Parent's Guide to Inspiring our Daughters to Achieve a Lifetime of Self-Esteem and Respect*, an Amazon top 10 pick for best parenting book of 2004, and as the recent 2006 winner of Woman's Day Magazine Award, Redbook's Strength and Spirit Award and the Heroes of Running Award presented by Runner's World, Barker has become a highly visible role model for women of ALL ages. Molly clearly is passionate about her work yet still claims that her most challenging task she has yet to do... inspire her own children, 10-year-old Hank and 7-year-old Helen to follow their own hearts and dreams so they can live healthy, thriving and peaceful lives.

Molly lives in Charlotte, and toys with the idea of one day doing another Ironman Triathlon, but in the meantime prefers running, cycling, swimming and hanging out with her own two kids and the girls in *Girls on the Run*.